This book belongs to

- -

Producer & International Distributor
eBookPro Publishing
www.ebook-pro.com

EASTER BASKET STUFFER MAZE BOOK
Preschool Activity Gift Book for Kids Ages 4-8 With 100+ Mazes
Featuring Rabbits, Easter Eggs, Flowers, and More

MADE EASY PRESS

Cover design: Maria Sokhatski

Contact: agency@ebook-pro.com
ISBN 9798879384123

Help the little snail get to her mother.

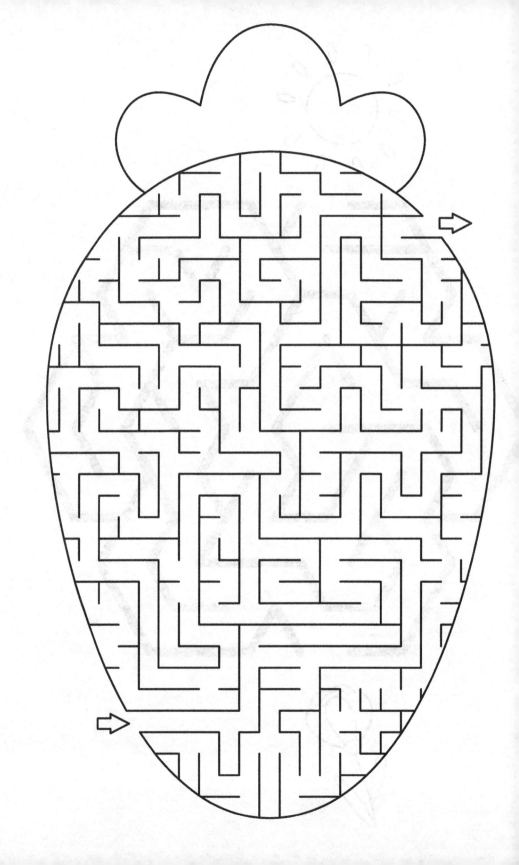

HELP THE GOSLING GET TO HIS MOTHER

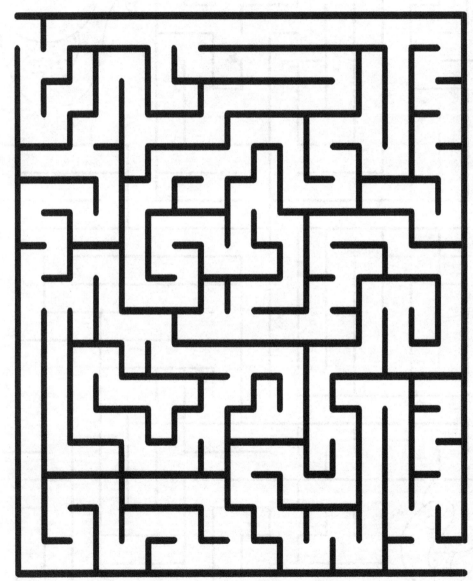

COLORING
FIND THE RIGHT PATH

Whose carrot?

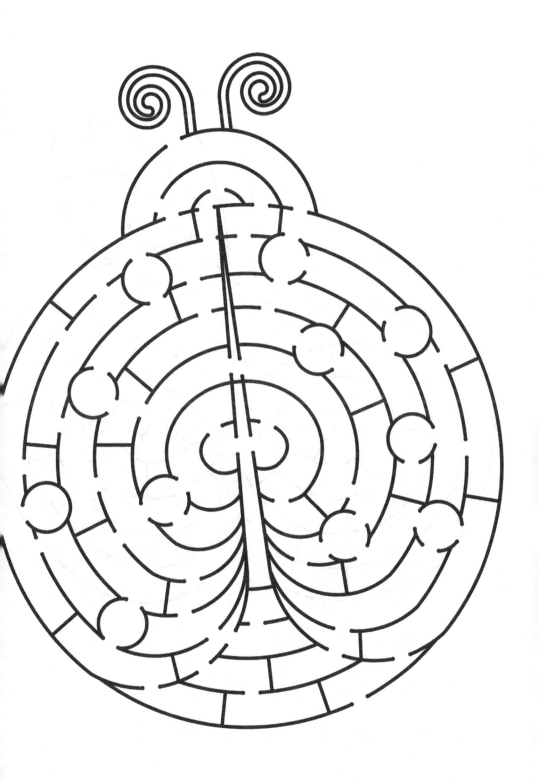

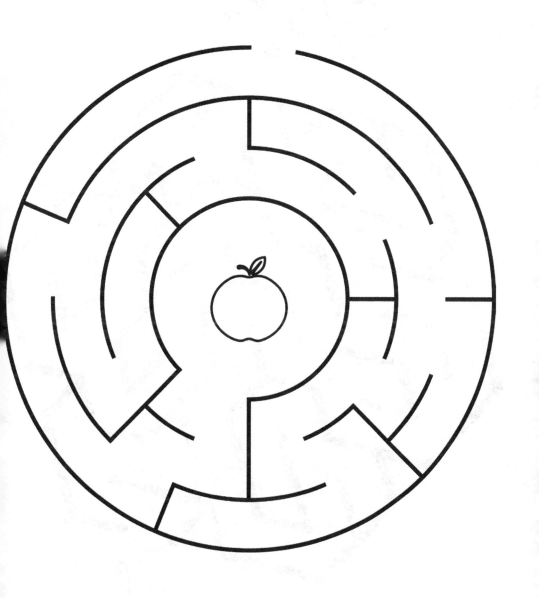

♡ WHOSE HOUSE? ♡

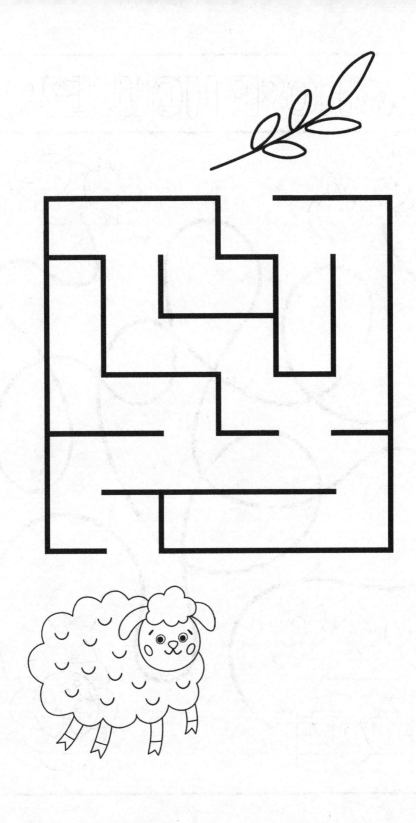

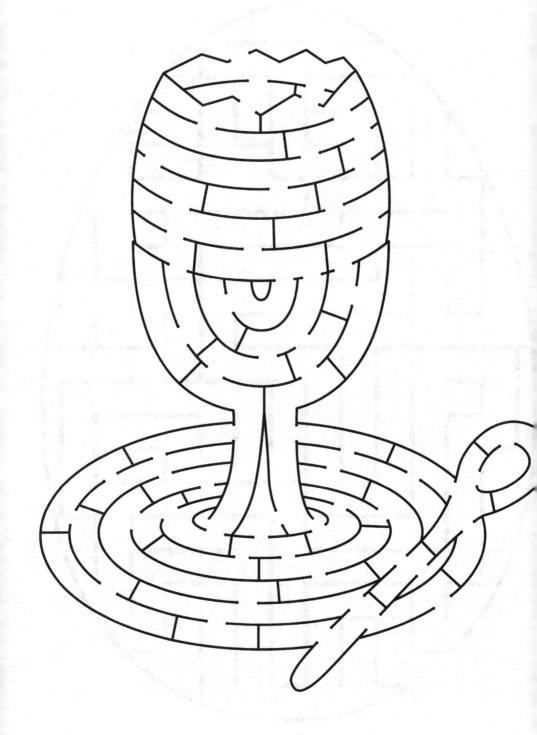

Whose egg is the farthest to roll down?

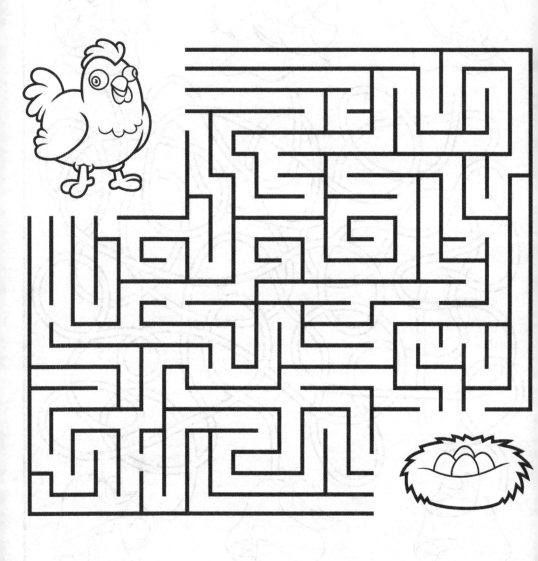

Help the pencils find the way out of the middle of the maze and paint all four eggs!

Help the rabbit collect all eggs

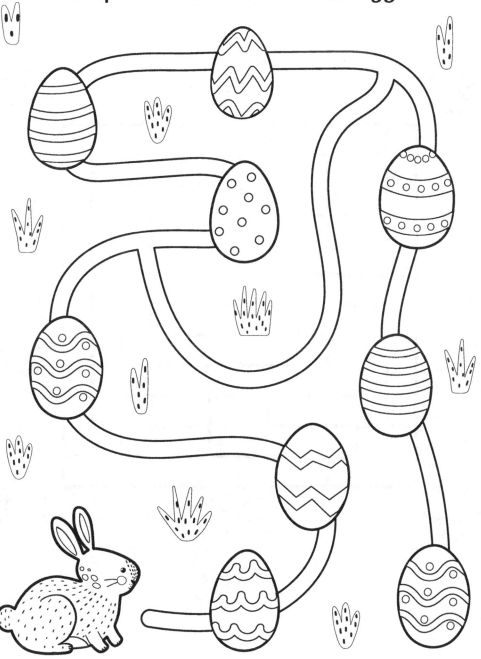

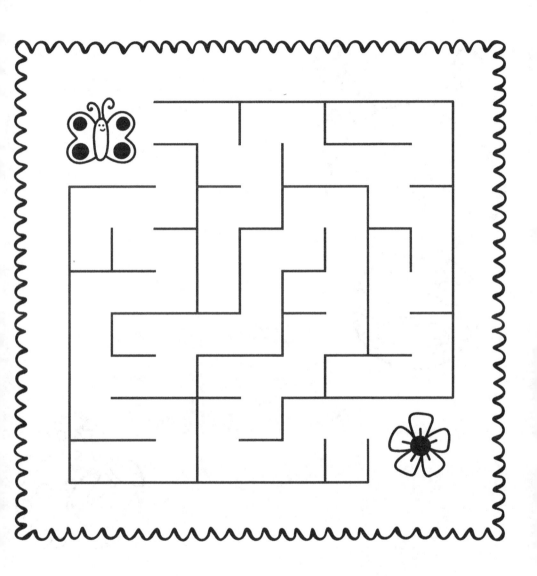

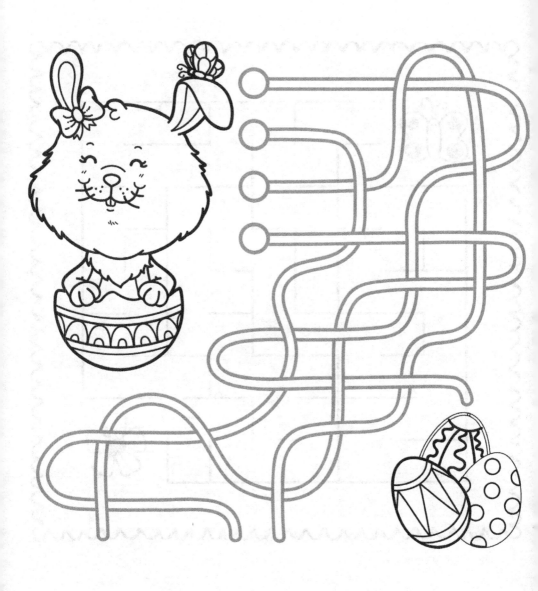

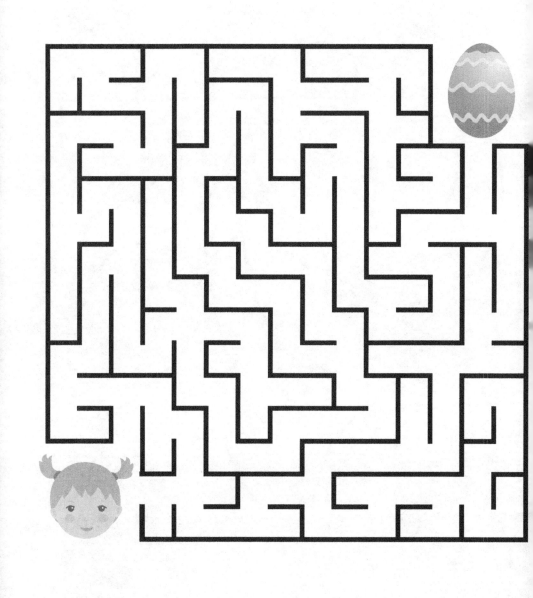

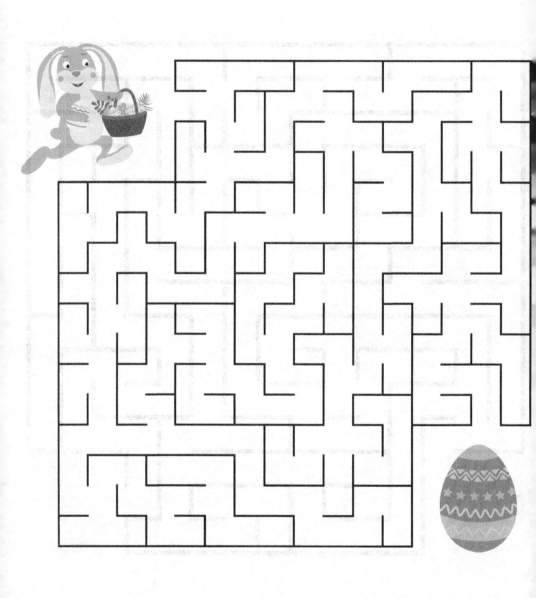

Which way leads to yummy carrots?

Help the cute chick to find Easter eggs

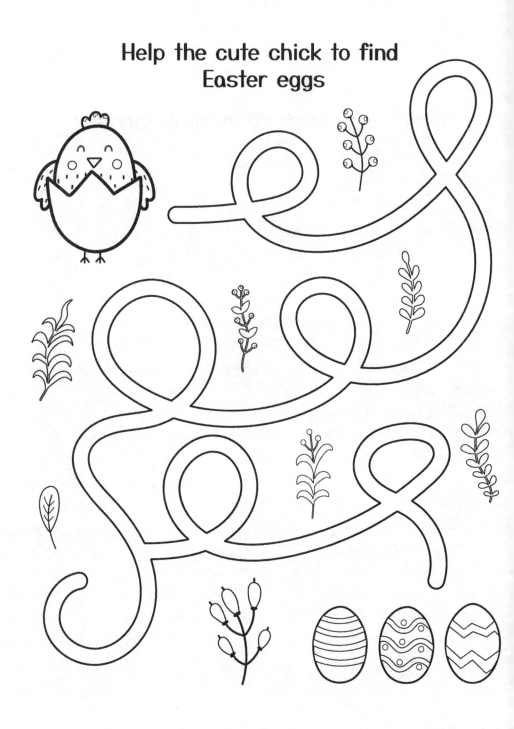

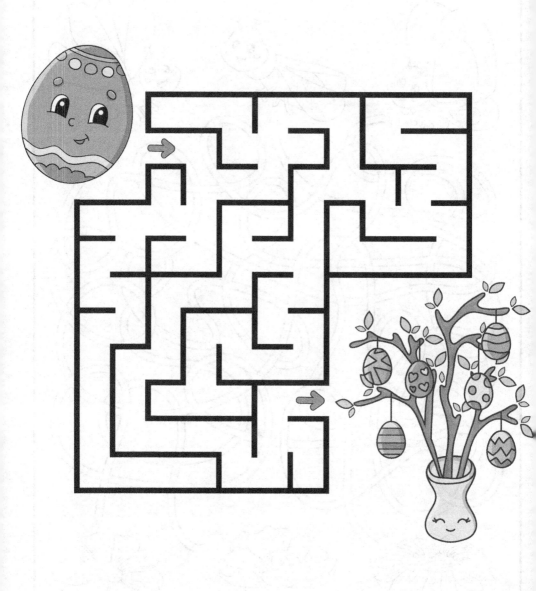

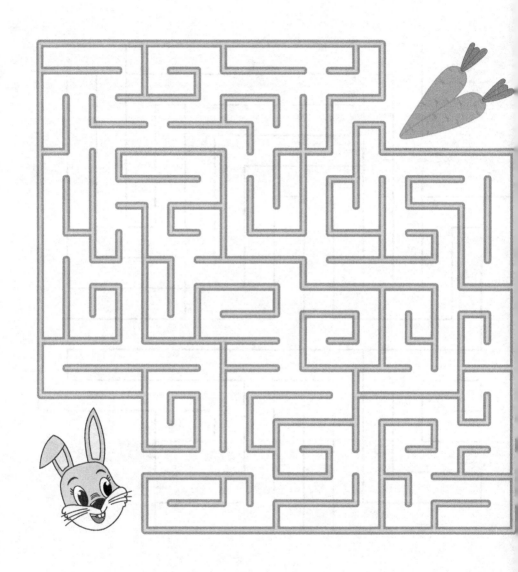

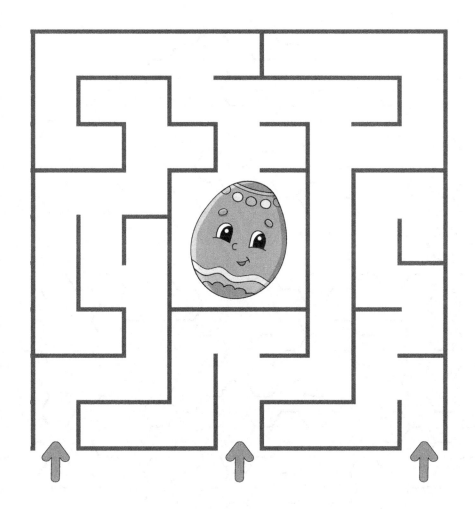

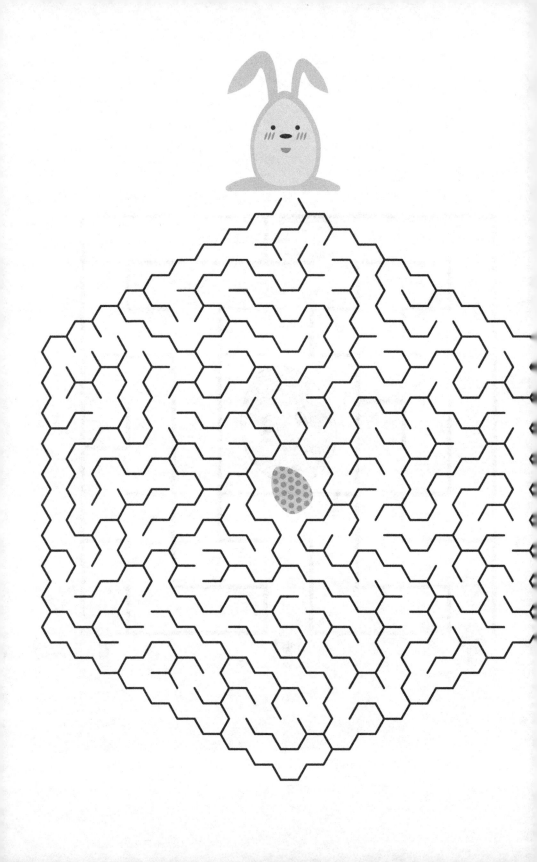

Help every pencil to find the way to the picture
in the middle of the maze and color all the eggs!

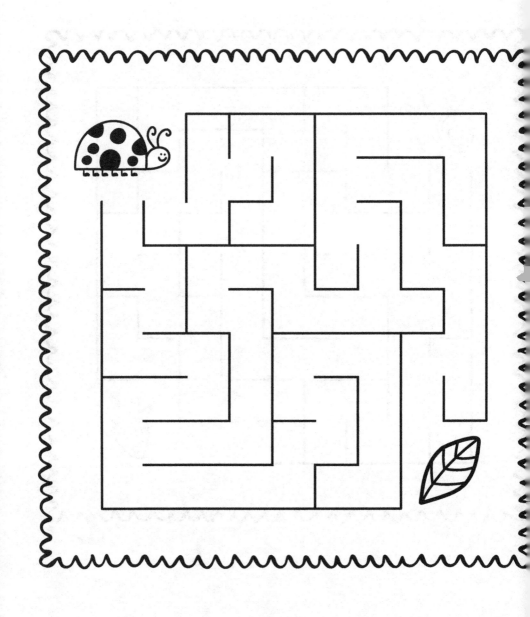

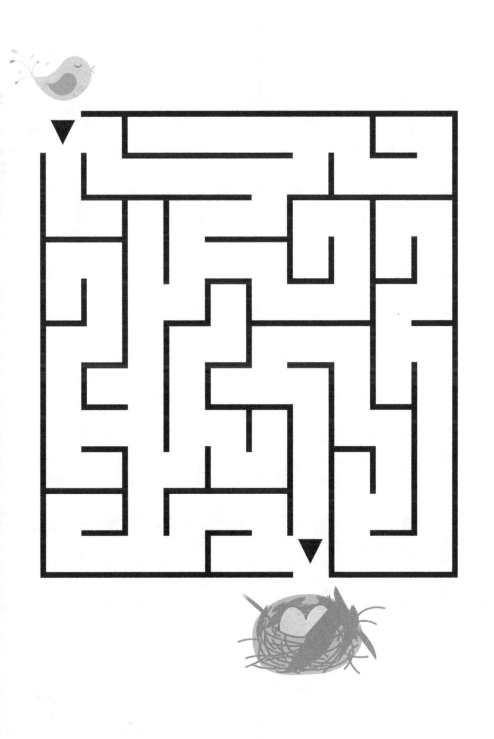

We hope you enjoyed

Easter Basket Stuffer Maze Book!

We'd appreciate it so much if you would consider
going to Amazon and leaving a review.

Your reviews help us bring you more fun,
family-friendly content like this book.

About Made Easy Press

At Made Easy Press, our goal is to bring you beautifully designed, thoughtful gifts and products.

We strive to make complicated things – easy. Whether it's learning new skills or putting memories into words, our books are led by values of family, creativity, and self-care and we take joy in creating authentic experiences that make people truly happy.

Look out for other books
by **Made Easy Press** here!

Made in the USA
Monee, IL
07 March 2025